THE SERMON ON THE MOUNT

VICTORIA

Text by Patricia Hunt

Illustrations by Eileen Madison

Printed in Italy for the Publishers

Peter Haddock Limited, Bridlington, UK

People loved to listen to Jesus. He told such wonderful stories. So wonderful, they have been remembered ever since.

Once he told a story about two men who each wanted to build a house. First of all, they looked around for a good place to build. The first man found a very good

place, for when he began to dig down, underneath the soil there was solid rock. It was very firm and soon he had built himself a very fine house. He was a wise man.

The second man did not think it important that the walls should be built on solid ground. He decided to build his house on sand. It looked nice too, but, as we shall see, this man was very foolish.

Both men soon finished their work and everyone had to agree that the houses did look very nice. The two builders were very pleased with what they had done. The houses looked strong and sturdy and the men felt

sure that they would last for a very long time. The men thought they had good reason to be proud of themselves.

While the sun shone, the houses did indeed look very beautiful. But one day there was a terrible storm. The rain came flooding down and it raged and beat upon the walls of the houses. Soon the land was flooded with water. The winds tore at everything — trees,

plants, people and buildings. The two men wondered whether their new buildings would ever survive. One of them did.

The house which was built upon rock was the one
which stood through the storm. Nothing could shake
it, because it had a very firm foundation. Foundations
are very important. You cannot see them because
they are underground. But it is the foundation which

gives a building its strength. If the foundation is weak, then the whole building is weak too. Sand is a very weak foundation for any building. As soon as the storm hit the house built on sand, it began to collapse.

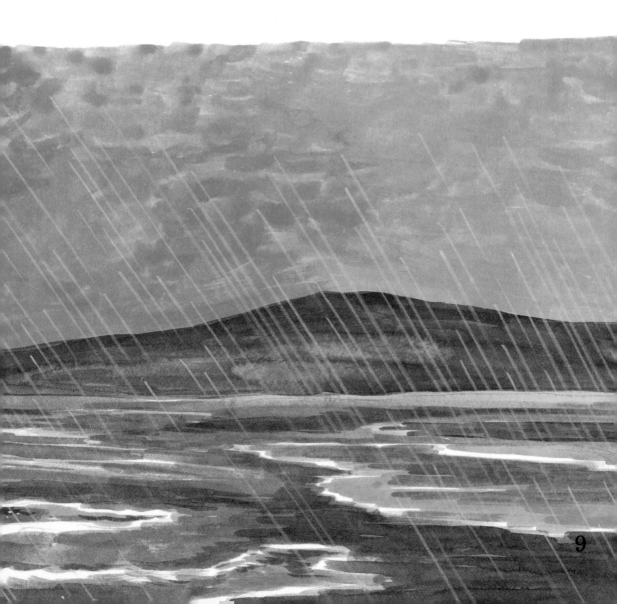

The storm did not rage for long before this house fell down. It came down with a terrible crash. It crashed because its foundations were weak. The wind and rain soon moved the sand and the house had no support.

After telling this story, Jesus said 'Listen to me and my teaching. Live the way I live. Then, no matter what happens to you in life, you will be strong. Your life will have a firm foundation.'

Jesus also told another story about two men. One looked at the other and said 'Please let me take that little speck out of your eye.'
But he could hardly see to do it, because he had a big log in his own eye! Jesus said 'First he must take the log out of his own eye, then he will be able to

see clearly to remove the speck from the other man's eye.'

By this Jesus meant that we must not always look for the wrong things that other people do, when we do worse things ourselves.

Jesus spoke a great deal about people who loved money, fine clothes, jewels and other riches more than anything else. They buy as many things as they can, but often they find that these things don't last.
Perhaps they go rusty, or moths get at the clothes, or thieves come and take everything away.
Jesus called such things 'treasures on earth'. Instead, He said, we should collect 'treasures in heaven', for these are things which can never be taken from us.

Such things as a kind, loving heart; lips which speak only what is good and true; eyes which look where help is needed; and a mind ready to think the best of people and to love God.

'When you give to the poor,' said Jesus, 'do not make a show of it. Give quietly, so that not even your best friend will know. But God will know, for He knows all. Again Jesus said 'Do not pray on a street corner, or

at a place where everyone can see you. Go somewhere you can be alone.' Here is the sort of prayer which Jesus would like us to pray:

Our Father which
art in Heaven,
Hallowed be thy name.
Thy kingdom come,
Thy will be done,
On earth as it is
in Heaven.
Give us this day our
daily bread;

And forgive us our
trespasses,
As we forgive them
that trespass
against us;
And lead us not
into temptation,
But deliver us from
evil.

'Our Father in heaven;
may your holy name be honoured;
may your Kingdom come;
may your will be done on earth
  as it is in heaven.
Give us the food we need.

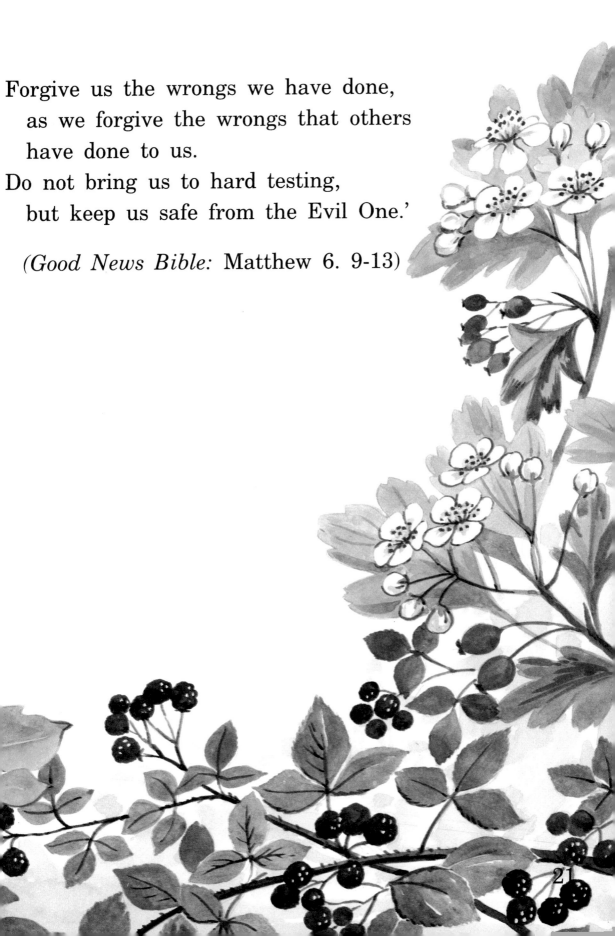

Forgive us the wrongs we have done,
  as we forgive the wrongs that others
  have done to us.
Do not bring us to hard testing,
  but keep us safe from the Evil One.'

(Good News Bible: Matthew 6. 9-13)

Now you can read the story again
and find these things

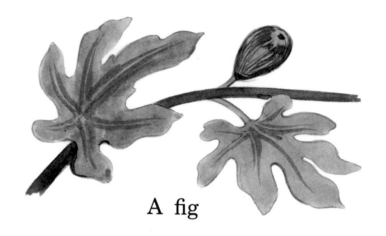

A fig

'treasures on earth'

The house built on sand

The house built on rock

The man with the log
in his eye

The ruins of the house built on sand